Booker T. Washington

Teacher, Speaker, and Leader

by SUZANNE SLADE

illustrated by SIRI WEBER FEENEY

PICTURE WINDOW BOOKS
Minneapolis, Minnesota

Special thanks to our advisers for their expertise:

H. Tyrone Brandyburg, Chief of Resource Education and Interpretation
Tuskegee Institute National Historic Site, Tuskegee Airmen National Historic Site
Selma to Montgomery National Historic Trail

Terry Flaherty, Ph.D., Professor of English
Minnesota State University, Mankato

Editor: Shelly Lyons
Designer: Hilary Wacholz
Page Production: Michelle Biedscheid
Art Director: Nathan Gassman
Associate Managing Editor: Christianne Jones
The illustrations in this book were created with acrylics and colored pencil.
Photo Credit: Library of Congress, page 3

Picture Window Books
5115 Excelsior Boulevard, Suite 232
Minneapolis, MN 55416
877-845-8392
www.picturewindowbooks.com

Printed in the United States of America.

 All books published by Picture Window Books
are manufactured with paper containing at least
10 percent post-consumer waste.

Library of Congress Cataloging-in-Publication Data
Slade, Suzanne.
Booker T. Washington : teacher, speaker, and leader / by Suzanne Slade ; illustrated
by Siri Weber Feeney.
p. cm. — (Biographies)
Includes index.
ISBN 978-1-4048-3977-9 (library binding)
1. Washington, Booker T., 1856-1915—Juvenile literature. 2. African
Americans—Biography—Juvenile literature. 3. Educators—United
States—Biography—Juvenile literature. I. Feeney, Siri Weber. II. Title.
E185.97.W4S58 2008
370.92—dc22
[B]   2007032875

Booker T. Washington was a great teacher and leader in education. He helped start the Tuskegee Normal School for Teachers, a school for African-Americans, in Alabama. Booker trained students to become teachers. He also believed students needed to learn job skills such as bricklaying and printing. With these skills, Booker believed students could succeed.

Through speeches and writings, Booker shared his ideas about learning. He raised money for his school and helped black and white people get along better.

This is the story of

Booker T. Washington.

Booker T. Washington was born a slave in 1856. He grew up on a Virginia farm with his mother, brother, and sister. They lived in a one-room cabin with dirt floors. Booker's mother was a farm cook. As a child, Booker did yard work and carried water to fieldworkers.

It was against the law in Virginia for slaves to attend school, so Booker could not go. At times, he walked to school with his owner's daughter and carried her books. When they arrived at the schoolhouse, Booker would take a quick peek inside. He wanted to go in and study, too.

7

When Booker was 9 years old, the Civil War (1861–1865) ended, and slaves were freed. His family moved to West Virginia. It took Booker and his family several weeks to walk most of the 200-mile (320-kilometer) journey.

When Booker was 9 years old, he began working
in a salt furnace in West Virginia. As he worked,
Booker dreamed of learning to read. At night,
Booker often looked at an old spelling book,
but he did not know what the letters stood for.

Soon a school for black children opened nearby. Booker worked
early in the morning so he could get to school by 9 a.m.

At 16, Booker left home to continue his education at Hampton Normal and Agricultural Institute in Virginia. Hampton Institute was a school that trained African-American students to become teachers. He graduated in 1875 and became a teacher.

In 1881, Booker was asked to be the principal of a new school in Alabama, the Tuskegee Normal School for Teachers. It was a school for training teachers. When it opened, the school had about 30 students. It had one small shack for a classroom. The shack's roof leaked when it rained, but Booker kept teaching as a student held an umbrella over him.

Every year, more students came to the Tuskegee school. Booker traveled around the country raising money for the school.

At first, Tuskegee Normal School was only for future teachers. But within two years, the school also had other classes, such as bricklaying and printing. Soon, the school's name became Tuskegee Normal and Industrial Institute.

By 1883, Booker and his students began making bricks. They used the bricks to build new buildings for the school. They also sold some of the bricks to earn money for the school.

Booker believed that if African-Americans worked hard, white people would begin to respect them. He believed that by gaining respect, African-Americans would also one day gain equality.

In 1895, Booker gave a famous speech in Atlanta, Georgia. In his speech, he said blacks and whites could be separate but could also work together for the benefit of all. After this speech, Booker was asked to speak all over the country. He had become a spokesman for African-Americans.

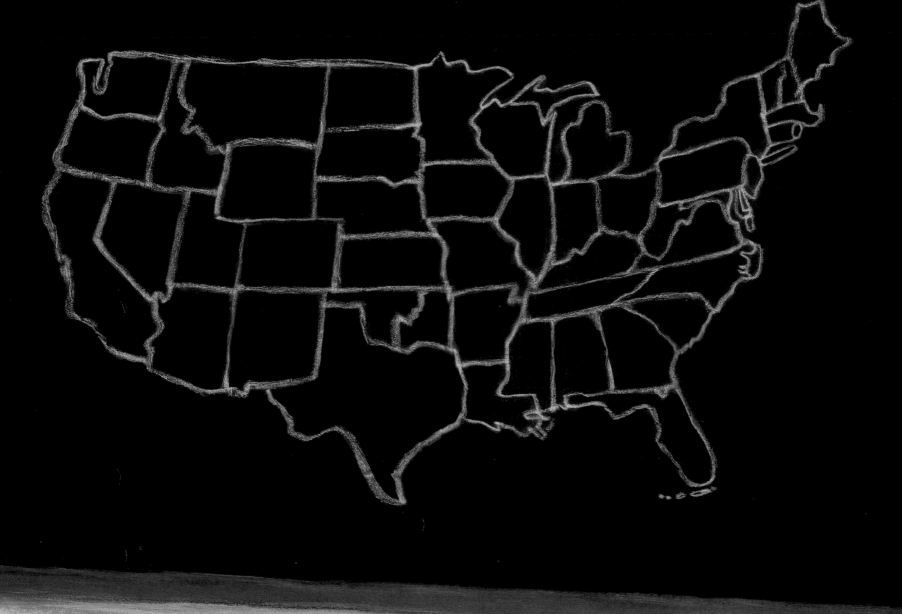

In 1900, Booker helped start the National Negro Business League. The aim of the group was to teach African-Americans about business. Branches of the National Negro Business League soon were started in many states throughout the country.

National
Negro
Business
League

19

In 1901, Booker wrote *Up From Slavery*.
In his book, he wrote about his life and ideas.
The book helped change some people's
beliefs about education and jobs for
African-Americans. It also brought
more money and students to
Tuskegee Institute.

Booker taught and worked for education until he died in his home in Tuskegee, Alabama, on November 14, 1915. He was 59 years old.

Booker T. Washington changed the lives of many people through education. As a spokesman in his community, Booker voiced his ideas about the importance of education and civil rights.

The Life of Booker T. Washington

1856	Born a slave in Virginia
1865	Freed from slavery when the Civil War ended; moved to Malden, West Virginia
1875	Finished classes at Hampton Institute and began teaching
1881	Opened Tuskegee Normal School for Teachers
1882	Married Fannie Smith
1883	Daughter, Portia, was born
1884	Fannie Smith died
1885	Married Olivia Davidson; son Booker T. Washington Jr. was born
1889	Son Ernest Davidson Washington was born; Olivia Davidson died
1892	Married Margaret Murray
1895	Gave his famous speech in Atlanta, Georgia
1900	Helped start the National Negro Business League
1901	Wrote a book about his life called *Up From Slavery*
1915	Died in his home at Tuskegee, Alabama, on November 14, at age 59

Did You Know?

~ Booker did not know the exact date of his birth. Slave owners did not keep records of slaves' birthdays. He also never knew who his father was.

~ When Booker died from an illness in 1915, he was buried at Tuskegee Normal and Industrial Institute. Today the school is called Tuskegee University.

~ Booker was the first African-American to dine at the White House. He was the guest of President Theodore Roosevelt on October 16, 1901.

~ Growing up, Booker T. Washington was simply called "Booker." When he learned that children at school had a last name, Booker said his was Washington. Booker later learned his mother had named him Booker Taliaferro. His name ended up as Booker Taliaferro Washington.

Glossary

civil rights — freedoms that every person should have

Civil War (1861–1865) — the battle between states in the North and South that led to the end of slavery in the United States

education — dealing with teaching and learning in schools; the process of learning in a school system

equality — being equal

plantation — a large farm where crops are raised by people who live there

salt furnace — a place where people processed salt

slave — a person who is owned by another person

23

To Learn More

More Books to Read

Braun, Eric. *Booker T. Washington: Great American Educator.* Mankato, Minn.: Capstone Press, 2006.

Frost, Helen. *Let's Meet Booker T. Washington.* Philadelphia: Chelsea Clubhouse, 2004.

Gosda, Randy T. *Booker T. Washington: A Buddy Book.* Edina, Minn.: Abdo Publishing, 2002.

McKissack, Pat and Frederick McKissack. *Booker T. Washington: Leader and Educator.* Berkeley Heights, N.J.: Enslow Publishers, 2001.

On the Web

FactHound offers a safe, fun way to find Web sites related to topics in this book. All of the sites on FactHound have been researched by our staff.

1. Visit *www.facthound.com*

2. Type in this special code:
   1404839771

3. Click on the FETCH IT button.

Your trusty FactHound will fetch the best sites for you!

Index

Look for all of the books in the Biographies series:

Abraham Lincoln: *Lawyer, President, Emancipator*
Albert Einstein: *Scientist and Genius*
Amelia Earhart: *Female Pioneer in Flight*
Benjamin Franklin: *Writer, Inventor, Statesman*
Booker T. Washington: *Teacher, Speaker, and Leader*
Cesar Chavez: *Champion and Voice of Farmworkers*
Frederick Douglass: *Writer, Speaker, and Opponent of Slavery*
George Washington: *Farmer, Soldier, President*
George Washington Carver: *Teacher, Scientist, and Inventor*
Harriet Tubman: *Hero of the Underground Railroad*
Jackie Robinson: *Hero and Athlete*
Marie Curie: *Prize-Winning Scientist*
Martha Washington: *First Lady of the United States*
Martin Luther King Jr.: *Preacher, Freedom Fighter, Peacemaker*
Pocahontas: *Peacemaker and Friend to the Colonists*
Sally Ride: *Astronaut, Scientist, Teacher*
Sojourner Truth: *Preacher for Freedom and Equality*
Susan B. Anthony: *Fighter for Freedom and Equality*
Thomas Edison: *Inventor, Scientist, and Genius*
Thomas Jefferson: *A Founding Father of the United States of America*